AMAZING ANIMALS

This edition published in
the United States in 1997
by World Book Inc.
525 W. Monroe
Chicago, IL 60661
in association with
Two-Can Publishing Ltd.

**For information on other World Book products,
call 1-800-255-1750, x 2238.**

ISBN: 0-7166-4501-7

Printed in Hong Kong

1 2 3 4 5 6 7 8 9 10 99 98 97 96

Design by Elizabeth Bell. Art directed by Catherine Page. Picture research by Debbie Dorman. Production by Lis Clegg.

Front cover photographs: Britstock IFA/Weststock M. Newman. Inserts: Ardea. Illustrations: Oliver Frey, Chris West.

Picture Credits:
Bruce Coleman Ltd. 7, 8, 17tc, 19c, tr, 25br, 27tr; OSF 8/9, 20/21c, 20br, bl, tr, 21tr; NHPA 9br, 21br; International Society of Cryptozoology 10/11; Ardea 11br, 16, 17t, bc, b, 19br, 20cl, 22, 23, 30b, 31tl, c, tr; London Zoo 14, 15tr; Hulton Deutsch 15br; Todd Peterson 24, 25bl; Kobal Collection 26/27; Magnum 27br; John Drysdale 28, 29tl, tr, c, cr, bl; Britstock IFA 29br.

Illustrations:
Chris West 4/5, 6, 12/13, 18, 26/27; Joe Lawrence 4/5, Woody 8, 9; Oliver Frey 14/15.

CONTENTS

FREAKY

The amazing Aussie animals that time forgot

Australia's vast continent of 2.9 million square miles is home to some of the world's oldest – and strangest – animals.

To understand the weird wildlife of Australia, we need to take a step back in time. Back 150 million years, in fact, to an age when dinosaurs roamed the earth.

AUSSIE ODDITIES

As you'll see from our chart below, animal life on earth has been changing for hundreds of millions of years. This process of change is called evolution. Creatures have had to evolve or adapt to survive other changes in the world. Changing climates and shifting seas can cause havoc for all wildlife – including humans! Creatures that cannot adapt themselves to cope with new conditions die out and become extinct.

There are some backwaters of the world where primitive animals have remained exactly as they were millions of years ago. Australia is one such place. It is home to two strange groups of primitive animals – monotremes and marsupials – which in other places developed into more advanced mammals.

SURVIVAL OF THE FITTEST

Monotremes are mammals that lay eggs. They first came into existence 150 million years ago, during the great dinosaur age. At that time, some reptiles were beginning to evolve into mammals. The earth's different continents were still joined together in one huge land mass.

Gradually, the land started to break up into the continents we know today. Africa and South America drifted away from each other, and Antarctica and Australia were cut off on their own.

On other continents, more developed kinds of mammals became the boss and eventually wiped out weaker creatures. But on the isolated islands of Australasia, a unique wildlife was able to develop all by itself.

Today only two varieties of monotreme survive, both native to Australasia. They are the duck-billed platypus and the echidna, or spiny anteater.

> **DID YOU KNOW?** Echidnas and platypuses are the only egg-laying mammals in the world. Both are protected by law.

▶ *The platypus's bill is strangely soft and leathery and contains very sensitive nerves. It uses its big beak to dredge the bottom of rivers for worms.*

ANIMAL EVOLUTION
Our chart shows how modern animals have developed through the ages.

5,000 million years ago

4,600 million years ago
The earth is born from a spinning cloud of hot dust and gases.

3,200 million years ago
The first living things grow in the seas covering the earth, leaving behind fossil remains.

700 million years ago
The first animals appear in the sea, such as jellyfish and sponges.

570 million years ago
The first shellfish emerge.

throwbacks

FREAK OUT!

If there were a prize for the weirdest animal in the world, the duck-billed platypus would win webbed-feet down. It looks as if this amazing mammal has been put together using pieces from lots of other animals: an otter's body, a beaver's tail, and, of course, a duck's bill. On top of all that, it lays eggs. No wonder scientists were convinced the freaky creature was a fake when, in the 18th century, a stuffed platypus was first brought to Great Britain!

What really makes the platypus and the echidna weird is that they have half-reptilian and half-mammalian characteristics. They both lay eggs, like reptiles. But like other mammals, the monotremes feed their young with milk from their bodies.

When the female echidna is ready to give birth, she grows a flap of skin on her belly, which

▲ *The echidna is covered in a spiky armor to protect it from enemies. When it's under threat, the echidna burrows quickly into the hard ground so that only the thorny tips of its spikes are visible.*

forms a pouch. As the egg is laid, the echidna pushes it into the pouch where it hatches after about 10 days.

---

500 million years ago
Fish as we know them appeared.

370 million years ago
Some fish leave the swamps to begin life on land, developing into amphibians.

180 million years ago
The first mammals appear. Two survivors of these early creatures are the duck-billed platypus and the echidna.

140 million years ago
Some reptiles grow feathers; the first birds take to the air.

100 million years ago
Marsupials – animals with pouches, such as kangaroos and wallabies – evolve.

50 million years ago
Primitive monkeys (lemurs) appear. One particular ape developed over a few million years into *homo sapiens*, or man.

MARVELOUS
Marsupials

Meet the strange creatures we call marsupials

Australia is known as the land of the marsupial. Marsupials are born in a very underdeveloped state. They have small brains and are less adaptable than other mammals – that's why the only marsupial to have survived anywhere else in the world is the American opossum.

Other famous marsupials include wallabies, kangaroos, cuddly-looking koalas, and the clumsy wombat. The Tasmanian devil is another oddball marsupial. It's a catlike creature that can swim long distances underwater. Famous for its bad temper, it is really no more aggressive than any other meat-eating animal.

Marsupials differ from other mammals because they are born too soon! Undeveloped, they must incubate outside their mother's body, in her pouch. Marsupials have taken on many different forms, some dwelling in trees like the koala, others in desert burrows. They have spread unchallenged throughout the grasslands of Australia.

However, not all of Australia's ancient wildlife has made it to the 20th century – and not all marsupials were cute and cuddly. Scientists have found the remains of a giant marsupial that looked like a cross between a gigantic guinea pig and a rhinoceros. Judging from the contents of its stomach, this ferocious creature would have been a ruthless hunter whose main prey was sheep. Yikes!

DID YOU KNOW? The Aboriginal word *koala* means "the animal that doesn't drink."

◀ *Although their young are known as cubs, koalas are often wrongly called bears. Their closest living relative is another marsupial, the wombat.*

▶ *The wombat looks like a small beaver. Although it chews on grass, roots, and tree bark, its teeth grow as fast as they are worn away!*

FRILLER!

This frilled lizard may look like a spine-chilling prehistoric star from the hit movie *Jurassic Park* – but this is science fact, not fiction! Strangely enough, *Chlamydosaurus kingii*, as our freaky friller is also known, may have helped provide the inspiration for the dual-crested spitting dilophosaurus of *Jurassic Park* fame. The big, colorful frill of the carnivorous movie star was created by the designers to make their meat-eating monster appear even more terrifying!

▲ This huge rock python swallows the gazelle it has squeezed to death.

Most snakes are carnivores and will eat almost anything they can catch. That means they will happily devour birds, frogs, lizards, rabbits, and rats. But some are fussy eaters: king cobras prefer to eat other snakes, for example.

GULP!

Snakes swallow their food whole, and most also eat their prey while it is still alive. Constrictors kill their prey by wrapping their bodies around their victim, suffocating it to death, and then swallowing it whole. Some large constrictors, such as the rock python (above), can swallow animals as large as antelopes in one gulp.

▲ S-S-Suppertime! This puff adder makes quick work of a froggy feast.

FANGS A LOT

★ There are about 2,400 species of snakes in the world, but only a small number can cause human deaths. Poisonous snakes have two hollow fangs in their upper jaws that they use to bite their victims and then inject poison into the wound. The main man-killers are Indian cobras, saw-scaled vipers, rattlesnakes, puff adders, and tiger and brown snakes. More than 10,000 people die from snakebite poisoning every year.

IT'S A WINDUP

★ Snakes don't move unless they really need to. When they do, they place their scales over rough parts of the ground to get a grip, then push and pull with their muscles. If they're on unstable ground such as sand, they move sideways by throwing their head to one side and then pulling up the rest of their body. This strange movement is called sidewinding.

▲ Sidewinders leave interesting trails in sand.

IT'S-S-S

OSCAR-WINNING PERFORMANCE
The hognose snake plays dead when threatened by an enemy. It rolls over on its back and lets its tongue hang out.

Watch out for the western rattler!

ON THE SLIDE
Come to grips with slippery snake facts

Fastest: The black mamba can move at nearly 7 miles per hour.

Spitters: The African "spitting" cobra can squirt venom into the eyes of an enemy 6½ to 8 feet away, causing temporary blindness.

Flyers: The gliding snake of southern Asia can "parachute" from one tree to another.

Hunger strike: An African Gaboon viper in a zoo once ate nothing for two and a half years.

Most deadly: These include the king cobra, black mamba, saw-scaled viper, and the taipan of Australia.

STARVATION DIET

★ Large snakes, such as boas and pythons, sometimes don't eat for more than a year. Some smaller ones can fast for six to twelve months. Snakes can do this because they are inactive for long periods of time. Being cold-blooded, they don't need much food to keep up their body temperature.

SNAKE, RATTLE, AND ROLL

Male rattlesnakes often battle it out over a female. They rear up and lunge at each other until one snake is forced down and retreats.

A FACT!
Everything you need to know about those amazing slithering sliders called snakes

BRAIN RATTLER
How does a rattlesnake make its famous whirring noise?

a) with its teeth
b) by clicking its tongue
c) by shaking its tail

Answer on page 32

9

SNAKES ALIVE!

If the very thought of snakes makes you shudder, imagine coming to grips with a 16-foot-long whopper!

Snakes come in a variety of sizes but when they are big – boy, are they big! The largest snakes in the world are the anaconda of South America and the reticulated python of Asia. Both can grow up to 30 feet long – that's roughly the length of the average bus!

The biggest snake ever found was a 33-foot-long reticulated python, but there are several stories of sightings of snakes measuring almost twice that length.

WANTED!

Large snakes are highly prized in some parts of the world. Teddy Roosevelt was so determined to track down a whopper that he offered a $1,000 reward to anyone who captured a snake over 30 feet long.

One expedition exploring the Orinoco River in Columbia came close to the reward, but they let their truly spectacular specimen slip away.

THE SNAKE HUNTERS

In 1944, Dr. Dunn, a snake specialist from Harvard University, told the tale of a huge reptile that had been shot in the water by one of the men on the expedition. His assistants dragged the super-long serpent onto the riverbank, where it measured in at 37 feet. The group then went off to have lunch. When they came back to take photographs, they found it had disappeared.

Where had their snake vanished to? One possible explanation is that the creature was only wounded and had managed to escape into the undergrowth. But could it be that this was just another tall story? The reward remains uncollected, though today it's worth a cool $50,000.

WATER WEIGHT

By the late 1940s, a Brazilian expert came to an important conclusion. After much research at the Sao Paulo snake institute, and on the evidence of several witnesses, Afranio do Amaral decided that 42-foot anacondas really did exist.

What does seem unlikely, however, is that any snake can exceed 50 feet. If an anaconda were longer and bulkier, it would almost certainly have to spend nearly all its life in water to support its weight.

▲ It took seven men to lift this awesome anaconda at the Bronx Zoo, New York nearly 100 years ago – and no wonder. The super-long serpent was the star of the show when he measured in at a massive 19 feet.

S-S-S-SCARED?

★ Snakes may be some of the most fascinating creatures in the world, but they're not exactly high on most people's popularity charts!

This may be because some slippery slitherers are poisonous, or maybe it's simply because they look so strange. But the truth is that most snakes are perfectly harmless to humans.

▲ **The shortest snake in the world is the thread snake. It only grows to a little over 4 inches long.**

About 5,000 animal species are endangered. This means that their numbers are decreasing and that they may die out and disappear forever. An animal species that has disappeared is called extinct. Until the 1980s, one species became extinct about every 100 years. Now, at least one species disappears every day.

UNDER THREAT
What drives a species to extinction?

Nowhere to live Every species needs its own natural surroundings, but many habitats are being destroyed by pollution, farming, and building.

Hunting and collecting Wild animals are sometimes captured to be sold as pets or hunted for valuable parts of their bodies.

Unwelcome strangers Animals introduced into the wild from another country can upset the natural balance and endanger existing species.

Human carelessness The increase in tourism means that more people are visiting unexplored areas and disturbing the natural wildlife there.

Take a world view of rare creatures under threat

THE RARE B

POLAR BEAR
Numbers are on the increase after it almost became extinct in the 1960s, but it's not out of danger yet.

CALIFORNIA CONDOR
This is one of the world's rarest birds, with about 60 left in captivity.

MEDITERRANEAN MONK SEAL
Just 500 of these shy seals remain in the Mediterranean waters around Greece.

KEMP'S RIDLEY SEA TURTLE
The most endangered of all marine turtles, there are now just 900 adult females left.

GOLDEN LION TAMARIN
Found in the rain forests of Brazil, this maned monkey is threatened by loss of habitat.

BLUE WHALE
Weighing as much as 30 elephants each, these massive creatures have been hunted almost to extinction.

SNOW LEOPARD

Hunted mainly for its beautiful fur, this rare cat lives in the high mountain ranges of Asia.

GIANT PANDA

Pandas need an awful lot of bamboo to eat and, sadly, there isn't that much around anymore.

CHINESE TIGER

Thought to be the species from which all other tigers evolved, there are fewer than 50 left.

YANGTZE RIVER DOLPHIN

Threatened by pollution, hunters, and dam-building, there are only about 300 of these dolphins remaining.

PHILIPPINE EAGLE

Only 35 of these birds are known to exist, although a baby Philippine eagle was born in captivity in 1992.

SIKA DEER

Famous for its whistling scream, this pretty spotted deer is still found in a few parts of Asia.

ASIAN ELEPHANT

Less than 40,000 of these majestic jumbos are around today.

SLOTH BEAR

Poachers hunt this bear to use its body in so-called "medicines." Fewer than 10,000 remain in the wild.

MOUNTAIN GORILLA

There are only about 600 gorillas left in the mountains of Central Africa.

AFRICAN ELEPHANT

Although ivory trade is supposed to be banned, there are only 600,000 of these elephants left.

NUMBAT

Once common over half of Australia, this rare marsupial can now be found only in the southwestern corner.

SUCCESS STORY

★ It's not all gloom and doom for endangered species. In 1830, there were 60 million American bison, but by 1894 hunters had reduced numbers to less than 100. Thanks to captive breeding, there are now more than 30,000 American bison in the United States and Canada.

UNCH

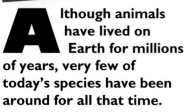
Weird and wonderful animals that are gone ... but not forgotten

Although animals have lived on Earth for millions of years, very few of today's species have been around for all that time.

As time passes, a species can survive only if it is in prime condition. The expression "survival of the fittest" means that only animals that are strong and well-adapted to their environment will flourish.

THE AGE OF MAN

Natural disasters and changes in climate have wiped out even the toughest species. But, sad to say, the human race is to blame for many of the losses in the animal kingdom. When humans appeared on Earth around two million years ago, the rate of animal extinction soared. We have hunted animals for their food, skins, and fur and destroyed many of their natural habitats.

Thankfully, things are now changing. Humankind is starting to fight for the survival of many endangered species before it is too late.

ANCIENT HUNTERS

One species that is gone for good is the saber-toothed tiger (right), which roamed Africa, Europe, and North and South America for nearly 40 million years. It was a ferocious hunter with curved, swordlike teeth about 8 inches long.

Attacking animals almost twice its size, this tiger would leap on their backs and sink in its supersharp teeth. It became extinct about 10,000 years ago, though experts cannot agree whether it was wiped out by man, climatic changes, or a mixture of both.

NO DODO

If it hadn't been for humans, the dodo might still be at large today. The dodo lived on the island of Mauritius in the Indian Ocean. It had never learned to fly because it had no natural predators – until man arrived.

In the 16th and 17th centuries, sailors came to the island and hunted the dodo for food. Their animals ate its eggs and it was soon completely wiped out – hence the saying, "As dead as a dodo!"

XTINCT

▲ ZEBRA CROSSING

This familiar-looking animal is a relative of the zebra. The quagga lived in large herds in South Africa until it became extinct in 1858. It, too, fell victim to human need as farmers hunted the species to extinction for its meat.

▲ MIGHTY MAMMOTH

It's rare that we can tell exactly what an animal looked like if it has been extinct for a long time, but scientists have been lucky with the mammoth. It was quite similar to the elephant of today, though "woolly" mammoths had shaggy hair. Early man hunted these enormous animals for their meat, fur, and huge, curved tusks.

Occasionally, these massive beasts fell into ravines to their death. Quickly covered with snow and frozen earth, these mammoths were kept in a kind of cold storage. Thousands of years later, when scientists unearthed them, the bodies were perfectly preserved for posterity, still covered with flesh and hair!

It's amazing the way that nature helps animals protect themselves from the danger of predators. Some animals have tremendous speed to help them outrun their attackers. Others have markings that help them blend in with their environment and remain invisible to would-be diners. And some have armor to make them a less appetizing lunch prospect.

Armor comes in all sorts of shapes and sizes and fends off predators in different ways. Some animals have thick, tough, and totally untasty skins. Despite being large, hippopotamuses may sometimes look like a tasty meal to a hungry crocodile. But their skin is so thick that not even a croc with powerful jaws can bite its way through!

SHELL SUITS

Other animals have their own personal protective suits. Crabs have tough outer skeletons, while hedgehogs and porcupines have spiky quills which no sensible animal would want to get stuck in its throat.

An armadillo's skin is covered in bony plates. And, as everyone knows, turtles, snails, and mussels simply close up shop and hide in their shells when danger looms.

ANIMALS IN ARMOR

Many creatures need a thick skin if they want to survive!

◄ A DEVIL OF A LIZARD

Terrifying as it looks, the moloch (or thorny devil) is really quite harmless – unless you're an ant! This peace-loving lizard is found in dry, sandy areas and only grows to 8 inches. But while it might be just the right size for a snake's snack, its prickly casing makes the idea of him as lunch pretty hard to swallow.

◄ THE PANGOLIN

★ The pangolin's overlapping scales of armor are made of keratin and are fused together into sheets. Keratin is the substance that makes up human hair and nails.

Pangolins have two clever ways of protecting themselves. They can squirt a nasty-smelling liquid at anything that might try to eat them. And, like porcupines, they are capable of curling themselves up into a ball, exposing only their hard, bony scales. Mother pangolins will sometimes even curl around their young to form a protective ball of armor to foil any predators.

SAFE BOX ►

★ A turtle can pull its head, legs, and tail into its shell, which acts as a secure fortress. A hinge-back tortoise can go one better. It can bend the back of its shell down to give it even more protection.

◄ THE SALTWATER CROCODILE

How big Saltwater crocs usually grow to about 16½ feet long and weigh up to 1300 pounds. The longest ever recorded was about 26 feet long.

Type of armor Its scales are joined together by layers of skin. These act like shingles to make an all-over suit of armor.

Where they live In the coastal rivers, swamps, and estuaries of India, the Philippines, New Guinea, and northern Australia.

Food These fierce, excellent hunters eat almost anything – including humans – but mostly fish, mammals, and birds. Hundreds of people are killed by saltwater crocodiles every year.

SPIKES? YIKES!

Porcupines can't move very fast so they need their prickly quills to scare off predators. If an enemy gets too close, the porcupine will rattle its quills as a spiky reminder!

MOM'S THE WORD

The weird and wonderful ways some animals take care of their babies

Bringing up baby in the animal kingdom means different things to different creatures.

Some animals are caring parents – they protect their babies and teach them survival skills. But most creatures don't take care of their offspring at all! Many fish, amphibians, and reptiles lay eggs and then abandon them. The eggs' chances of survival are slim, which is one of the reasons so many of them are laid in one batch. The leatherback turtle lays up to 100 eggs at one time.

Not all fish lay eggs, however. The lemon shark gives birth to live babies – as mammals do – and sometimes there are up to 19 pups in one litter! And of course, not all mammals give birth. The duckbilled platypus and the spiny anteater (or echidna) both lay eggs, even though they are classified as mammals.

BORN TO RUN

A baby giraffe enters the world quickly. Mom gives birth standing up, watching for danger on the horizon. In just a few minutes, the young giraffe is tottering on long, shaky legs toward its mother. Within hours it is running and playing alongside her – with potentially the most dangerous phase of its life now over. A zebra mare can delay giving birth for several days. If she weren't able to time her act of birth in this way, her newborn foal would be more likely to fall prey to lurking predators.

IN THE POCKET

A baby kangaroo, or joey, couldn't survive from birth without special care from Mom. Her pouch is the perfect place to spend up to 11 months in safety.

A joey spends just 37 days forming inside its mother. When it is born, it crawls up the front of its mother's body to the protection of her freshly cleaned pouch.

ROOM FOR RENT

Born just one inch long (that's roughly the size of a cashew nut), the blind, deaf joey latches on to Mom's nipple. This then swells up inside the baby's mouth so that even when Mom starts bouncing around, the baby won't be shaken loose.

Feeding on Mom's milk, the joey soon grows big enough to be able to peek out from the pouch. Only when it is six months old will it climb out and learn to hop. And at the first sign of danger, the young joey will climb back into the pouch, well out of harm's way.

Finally, toward the end of its first year, the young kangaroo is too big to squeeze back into its mother's pouch. Less than one day later, its mother will give birth to another baby, which immediately crawls up into the vacant space!

Some cuckoos lay a ▶ single egg in a smaller bird's nest. When it hatches, the young cuckoo pushes the other eggs out of the nest. Its foster parents instinctively bring up the young bird as their own

18

▲ My two moms! A female sea horse places her eggs in a pouch on the male's abdomen. Then it's Dad who takes care of them until they hatch.

THE YOUNG ONES

★ A baby kangaroo is called a joey. Do you know what the offspring of these animals are called?
a) hare
b) swan
c) cheetah ▼

Answers on page 32

▲ Hopalong partners – kangaroo mom with a joey in her pouch

READING THE SIGNS

Go away! Come here! Watch out! Can you crack the code of animal language?

Animals communicate with one another in all sorts of ways.

Through their movements, facial expressions, appearance, and sound, animals can show fear, anger, or pleasure, attract a mate, and alert others to danger.

Meerkats (shown below) are

very sociable little creatures. They do everything in groups, from defending their territory to playing or sunbathing in the desert. Young, unmated females take charge of the meerkat babies while the mothers go in search of food for their young.

Standing upright, the nursemaids use their tails as a third leg and will scan the horizon for possible signs of danger – predators such as snakes or jackals. A single alarm call can send the whole meerkat group scurrying underground to safety.

STOP BOUNCING AROUND!

Messages can also be exchanged between different species. Impalas (pictured below) can jump several feet into the air when they are pursued by predators – strange when you realize that these great vertical leaps actually slow the animals down.

So why do they do it? It could serve as a kind of alarm for the rest of the herd, but that's not the only reason. The sight of their quarry leaping into the air also confuses predators such as lions, making it difficult to select a target. When faster, slicker hunters such as cheetahs are in pursuit, impalas don't waste time and energy bouncing – they run for their lives!

COLOR CODING

Animals use color for a variety of purposes, but one of the most common is to attract a mate.

On the Galapagos Islands, there are three species of booby bird – which could be

▲ **Feet *first* with the booby bird**

very confusing! But each species has adapted to make itself instantly recognizable with different colored feet. One species has green feet, one has red, and one has blue. As a male courts a female, he will proudly show her his feet to let her know that he's her type!

EARS HOW

Relaxed ears When a tiger is resting and relaxed (above), its ears point sideways and slightly forward.

Rotated ears When a tiger is angry (below), it will rotate its ears so that the backs of the ears face forward to reveal a white spot ringed with black. This shows that the tiger is agitated.

◄ At night, wolves keep in touch with their pack by howling as they roam.

▲ For the mandrill monkey, color is a sure sign of importance. The male mandrill's bright blue face makes him stand out as the leader of his group.

PERFECT

Beautiful birds with their own technicolor dreamcoats!

▼ Rainbow bright The rainbow lorikeet warns other lorikeets to keep away from its territory by performing a special dance of hopping and preening. Sure enough, other birds soon get the message and scram!

> There are more than 100 billion birds on our planet.

Birds have been lords of the air for millions of years, but their success in the skies is no secret. They have the best flying equipment you can imagine – wings and feathers.

A bird's wings are made up of several overlapping rows of feathers. These wings provide the lift needed to take off, and by flapping them in midair birds can keep themselves aloft.

LIVING COLOR

But feathers have other uses than just flying. They can also be unfurled to attract a mate or flapped to frighten enemies.

Some birds' feathers are so colorful that they look as if they've been dipped in paint. In South America, green-winged and scarlet macaws live together in large colonies. To our eyes, they all look the same, but each bird has a special pattern on its wings that helps other macaws tell who's who.

Male peacocks fan out their bright tail feathers to impress females. Often, male birds are bright and flashy – like pheasants and Sri Lankan junglefowl – while the females are a dull brown color. The females' color acts as camouflage so that they can sit on their eggs without being seen by predators.

GROUND BOUND

Just because a bird has feathers doesn't mean it can fly! Some, such as the ostrich and the cassowary, lost the ability to fly eons ago. But they do have other talents to make up for it. The ostrich, for example, is the largest bird on Earth. With its powerful legs it can sprint at speeds of up to 40 miles per hour. What a way to go!

plumage

◀ **Hummingbirds** are the lightest birds – some weigh a fraction of an ounce. They beat their wings so fast (up to 80 times a second) that they can hold themselves completely still in the air – and some can even fly backward!

▲ **Gouldian finches** These small, tropical birds are just $4\frac{1}{2}$ inches long. They live in small flocks on the open grassland of northern Australia.

◀ **African crowned crane** This bird has a spectacular display dance routine. It starts with a fast-stepping walk, then leaps into the air, flapping its wings like crazy. As the excitement mounts, it picks up sticks and tosses them into the air.

Feathers are made of keratin, the same substance found in human hair and nails.

▲ **Golden bowerbird** To make their bowers more attractive to females, the male birds will often lay bright objects such as shells, orchids, or berries on beds of moss at the entrance.

The Australian Victoria riflebird ▶ does an amazing dance routine to attract a mate. He shuffles up and down on a branch, flashing his green breast feathers and his bright blue feet.

Faced with danger, some animals stand their ground and fight for their lives. Others escape by running away. But this silly billy just keels over!

FAINTING ★GOATS★

If there were a prize for the bravest member of the animal kingdom, one thing is for certain – the incredible fainting goats would not win.

When a fainting goat is startled or surprised, its whole body freezes up, making it fall down, legs in the air. It's not just pretending to be dead, hoping to fool the enemy, it's paralyzed by fear – literally, "scared stiff."

This fainting is actually a sudden tensing up of all the goats' muscles. It's caused by an unusual gene in their bodies. Usually a faint lasts for just a few seconds and then the goat is up on its feet again –

at least until the next time it's frightened!

The amazing goats come from the Midwest. They are very rare – which is hardly a surprise. Every time they are attacked in the wild they flop right into the predator's jaws. But this fact also explains why the goats were once very useful.

The first known fainting goats belonged to a drifter named Tinsley who arrived in Tennessee in the 1880s. He sold his herd to a farmer, who used them as a decoy to protect his sheep.

When the flock was attacked by wild dogs or coyotes, the sheep would run away. The goats, on the other hand, would go nowhere. So instead of chasing the valuable sheep,

the attackers happily settled for easier pickings.

In some ways, fainting goats look like other types of goats. Look closely, though, and you'll see that their eyes bulge out and they have big ears that stick out from the sides of their heads.

These nearly-extinct goats are now making a comeback. Not, however, to sacrifice themselves protecting sheep but as family pets. They're already so popular there's even a Fainting Goats' Appreciation Society – no kidding!

★ **For more information on fainting goats, write to Deborah Lipsky, RR4, Box 234, Houlton, ME 04730.**

▲ *Out cold – but not for long. The goats' fainting spells usually last a few seconds, then they're back on their feet.*

PLAYING POSSUM

★ **Not all animals are as fainthearted as the fainting goats. But some have adapted all kinds of ways to confuse their predators and survive some very sticky moments!**

The Virginia opossum (below right), for example, is a hardy marsupial scavenger that needs to be continuously on guard for signs of danger. But should it be cornered by the enemy, this largest of all opossums has a clever emergency plan – it lies down and pretends to be dead!

Amazingly, the ploy often works. But it's not just opossums that use this tactic in moments of grave danger. For some time, it was thought that "playing possum" was the safest way for humans to behave should they encounter a bear. But this is actually a myth and not sound advice. After all, most bears are big meat-eaters and may be dangerous.

"IF I COULD TALK

Dr. Dolittle was fluent in creature-speak, but that was just make-believe... or was it?

Back in 1920, author Hugh Lofting wrote a book about an amazing animal-lover named Dr. Dolittle who spent his time traveling the world over, talking to all kinds of creatures, great and small.

Strange as it may sound, serious scientists have also tried to communicate with animals.

Of course, humans can't talk to animals in the way that we might talk to one another. But because our closest relatives in the animal world are apes, apes seemed a natural place to begin.

ANIMAL TALK
In the 1960s, animal researchers set about the task of trying to teach chimpanzees to talk. Of all the apes, chimps are most like humans. They live in similar social groups and they are highly intelligent.

At first, scientists tried to get chimps to speak using words, but no chimp managed to say more than four words. This wasn't a sign that they were lazy or stupid, though – they simply have different vocal chords from humans.

The big breakthrough came when a husband and wife team of scientists, the Gardners, decided to teach their chimps American Sign Language (ASL).

This is the same language of signing with hand movements that many deaf people use.

After four years of hard work, the Gardners managed to teach a female chimp named Washoe 132 different signs. Now Washoe could communicate with them by telling them when she was hungry or wanted to play. She could also understand when they asked her things in sign language. She even talked to herself when she thought no one was watching!

TALKING FAMILIES
Soon the Gardners had a whole group of chimps and their babies using sign language all the time, even among each other. They started making up words themselves by using different combinations of signs they already knew – for example, they called a swan a "water bird." Washoe herself taught her own son to use more than 50 different words in sign language.

There have been other experiments in talking to apes. Some chimps have been taught to use boards with more than 256 symbols on them. Each symbol represents a different word and scientists and chimps touch the symbols to make up sentences. Not quite what Dr. Dolittle had in mind perhaps, but it works!

Dr. Dolittle could speak several languages – incl

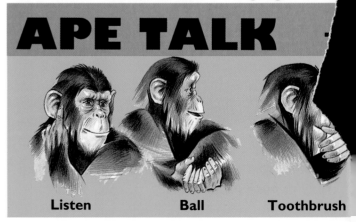

APE TALK

Listen   **Ball**   **Toothbrush**

REPEAT AFTER ME

★ If apes are such smart animals, how come less intelligent creatures such as parrots can talk when apes can't?

The answer is that parrots and birds like them are simply mimics. This means they copy the sounds they hear, although they cannot understand what they are saying.

The best talkers are African gray and Amazon parrots (above). Not only can they copy the sound of the human voice through constant repetition, they can also imitate the sound of a telephone ringing or a dog barking. Talk about confusing!

hant!

mps use these signs to "speak"

Bird   **Eat**   **Drink**

Chimps can communicate, but they can't say words.

SNAP HAPPY

A picture perfect look at some amazing animals

IT'S A FAM

Animals have been on Earth in one form or another for about 700 million years. Today, there are millions of different kinds of animals, but they can all be divided into seven different groups.

MAMMALS ▶

Mammals are found all over the world. There are about 4,500 species, including rodents, primates, marsupials, cats, bats, and human beings. All mammals have the following characteristics:

● warm blood, which means they can keep their bodies at a constant temperature
● hair or fur on their bodies
● the ability to suckle their babies
● a skull and backbone

Tigers are mammals that have been hunted for their f

Reptiles such as the rattlesnake are cold-blooded.

REPTILES ▲

Until 65 million years ago, enormous reptiles – the dinosaurs – ruled the earth. Today, there are about 6,500 kinds of reptiles. Reptiles are cold-blooded and they need to live in warm climates to keep their bodies at a constant temperature. The reptile family includes snakes, lizards, crocodiles, and turtles. Most reptiles have the following characteristics:

● scaly, waterproof skin
● the ability to lay eggs with tough, protective shells
● good vision

◀ AMPHIBIANS

Amphibians have adapted to live on land and in water. There are about 4,000 different species of amphibians including frogs, toads, newts, and salamanders. Most amphibians have the following characteristics:

● they live near water because it's their natural breeding ground
● their skin does not have scales
● they are cold-blooded

Red-eyed amphibian: the Panama tree frog

Y AFFAIR

There's no confusing which type of animal the hummingbird is.

Insects are by far the largest group of creatures on Earth. A million have already been identified, and scientists think there are between 1 million and 10 million species still undiscovered. The insect family includes ants, beetles, bees, butterflies, flies, and lice.

All insects have:
- three pairs of jointed legs
- cold blood
- a protective outer coating called an exoskeleton
- a head with eyes and antennae
- no lungs – they breathe through holes in their sides

The stunning peacock butterfly is an insect – not a bird!

BIRDS

All birds have wings and feathers, though some of them have lost the ability to fly. There are about 9,700 kinds of birds, found all over the world, from the freezing polar lands to hot, tropical rain forests. They greatly vary in size, from the tiny hummingbird to the enormous ostrich.

All flying birds have:
- waterproof feathers covering their bodies
- a streamlined shape to help them move smoothly through the air
- bones that are partly hollow to make them as light as possible for flying

An arachnid with a sting in its tail – the scorpion

◀ ARACHNIDS

These have eight legs and include all kinds of creepy crawlies, from spiders to mites to scorpions.

All arachnids have:
- four pairs of legs
- one to six pairs of simple eyes
- no wings
- a body made up of just two main parts
- no antennae

◀ FISH

Fish live underwater in oceans, rivers, lakes, and ponds. They are cold-blooded, which means that they cannot change their own body temperature. There are about 21,700 different species of fish, including sharks, sea horses, and eels.

All fish have:
- backbones – they are vertebrates
- scaly, waterproof skin
- gills, which they use to absorb oxygen from the water around them
- fins and a tail to steer them through the water

Did you know that the sea horse is a type of fish?

WHAT A MIX-UP!

Some animals have characteristics common to more than one group. Take the duck-billed platypus, for example. Unlike most other mammals, it lays eggs yet it suckles its young with milk from its mammary glands and is therefore officially classed as a mammal.

INDEX

ANSWERS TO QUESTIONS

Brain Rattler – page 9: c) **The Young Ones** – page 19: a) leveret b) cygnet c) cub